# GET WELL JOHNNY

## Book 2: Superfoods Are Super Fun!

## By Dr. Pooch

## Illustrations by Cuzzin' Dave

Dr. Pooch Publishing, LLC
drpooch.com

ISBN: 978-0-9964667-5-2

DISCLAIMER: Dr. Pooch is NOT a medical doctor. Therefore, the information
within this book is for educational purposes only. It should not be used
as a substitute for professional medical advice, diagnosis or treatment
regarding your or your child's well-being.

For more info: visit drpooch.com

This book is dedicated to Dave "Cuzzin' Dave" Rodriguez, who lost his battle with cancer during the making of this book series. He was a one-of-a-kind guy with a great sense of humanity and humor.

Before the "Get Well Johnny" series, Cuzzin' Dave worked on Charlie Brown, Teenage Mutant Ninja Turtles and more. May his memory be honored by any who've gained insight from the wisdom within this book.

*May you rest in peace, Cuzzin' Dave.*

# NOTE TO PARENTS

Imagine you were able to surpass your daily nutritional intake and provide life-changing benefits to your body by eating or drinking a heaping teaspoon of your favorite Superfood everyday. Superfoods really are super fun and nutritionally packed with condensed minerals, vitamins, proteins, amino acids and more.

Superfoods are proven safe by millennia of human usage and have absolutely no side effects. Hippocrates, the father of modern Western medicine said over 2000 years ago: "Let thy food be thy medicine and thy medicine be thy food." The medicinal value of a Superfood is proven by its ability to boost immunity, fight off bad cholesterol, and prevent obesity, diabetes, inflammation, anemia, cancer and much more.

Superfoods are non-processed, real, natural foods. They are still in a high energetic state and thus invigorate bodies when needed and help them relax when appropriate. Superfoods are the perfect way to balance your and your child's diet by cutting sugar cravings and putting nutrients back in the body rather than stripping them away.

Incorporate Superfoods in your daily meals. Processed foods lack mineral density and, in turn, they become very harmful to health. It is imperative for your family's health to make Superfoods a part of your daily diet.

-Dr. Pooch

Superfoods are super fun; they're super good for everyone.
To be super strong, not super weak,
you must eat what superheroes eat.

Superheroes eat açai, broccoli and kale,
to be alert and ready every day without fail.

Superfoods are super fun; they're super good for everyone.
To be super sharp and just get smarter,
eat the foods that feed the doctor.

Doctors eat asparagus, quinoa and peas
to be aware and keen when diagnosing disease.

Superfoods are super fun; they're super good for everyone.
To have super strength and not be beat,
eat what all pro athletes eat.

Pro athletes eat sea vegetables, hemp seeds and flax
to make sure that, win or lose, they can push it to the max.

Superfoods are super fun; they're super good for everyone.
To be super wise and the keenest judge,
eat what every lawyer does.

Lawyers drink Moringa tea, eat walnuts for Omega-3's, eat coconuts and blueberries for healthy brain activity.

Superfoods are super fun; they're super good for everyone.
To get straight A's, 1st grade to College,
eat Superfoods on your quest for knowledge.

They're high in vitamins and
a great mineral source.
They have plenty of enzymes and protein,
of course.

10

They give your body all that you need,
to give you the tools so you can succeed.

Boys and girls become super teens
that are super cool and do super things.

Eating Superfoods puts you in a super mood,
when you're feeling super good you're a super dude.

So eat and drink all the best,
nothing more and nothing less.

Because once you've had one taste of it,
you'll always be the super-est!!!!

BAOBAB TREE

**BAOBAB FRUIT** is from an ancient tree found in Africa that can live more than 6000 years! Its fruit is unique because it dries on the branch! Baobab is full of antioxidants and very high in vitamin C! This makes it very good for treating and preventing colds! Try it as a pudding or drink, just add a healthy sweetener!

BRAZIL NUTS

**BRAZIL NUTS** are the highest source of selenium in the plant kingdom! Selenium is an essential mineral that is important in preventing cancer. Brazil nuts are packed with antioxidants and immune boosting properties. They contain healthy fats, which keep the heart healthy and are a good source of amino acids to give you energy. Add 2-3 nuts to your daily salad and watch this Amazonian superfood transform your health!

GOLDEN BERRIES

**GOLDEN BERRIES** are antioxidant powerhouses! Antioxidants keep the body young and free of chronic disease. Golden Berries are awesome at fighting inflammation. This means they're good for blood pressure, arthritis, heart disease and more. These superfood berries contain carotenoids that strengthen the eyes and contain a rich source of nutrition to the kidneys and liver helping them detoxify.
Eat this superfood fruit daily to prevent diabetes from affecting you or your loved ones.

HEMP SEEDS

**HEMP SEEDS** are not only a perfect protein containing all amino acids, but this ancient food is packed with vitamins and minerals to ensure a blast of nutrients to the whole body! Hemp seeds are safe for kids to consume and are a perfect milk replacement. These super seeds are the most nutritionally complete food in the world and contain a perfect balance of omega 3's and 6's to feed the brain!

KIWIS

**KIWIS** are fuzzy fruits that are extremely high sources of vitamin C, which protects the immune system and skin. Kiwis can help in preventing asthma and because of their green color provide chlorophyll, which is pure sunlight plant energy. Kiwis are good for colon health and have lots of fiber to assist in regular bowel movements. This superfood fruit just may be one of the most nutrient dense fruits around!

# SuperFood Pudding

**HI, MY NAME IS ALMOND RAW AND TOGETHER WE'LL MAKE FUN, GREAT TASTING RAW RECIPES!**

## WHAT YOU'LL NEED IS:
- 1 Avocado
- ½ Tablespoon Virgin Coconut Oil
- 2 Cups of Spring Water
- 7 Dates (pitted)
- 3-4 Fresh Basil Leaves
- ½ Cup of Hemp Seeds (optional)
- Blender

ALMOND RAW

## INSTRUCTIONS:
1. Place all the items into a high-speed blender.
2. Blend until homogeneous.
3. Enjoy cold or room temperature
Serves 2.

## HEALTH TIP

THIS IS A GREAT WAY TO INCORPORATE SUPERFOODS INTO YOUR DAILY LIFE. TAKE AN INDIVIDUAL SPIN ON THE RECIPE.

REMEMBER: SUPERFOODS ARE SUPER FUN!

# CIRCLE THE SUPER FOOD

CACAO

BERRIES

BURGER

SODA

SWEET POTATOES

BROCCOLI

WHICH OF THESE ARE SUPERFOODS, AND WHICH ARE UNHEALTHY?

## HELP MARY BERRY
## FILL IN THE BLANKS

WHAT KIND OF BERRIES DOES MARY LIKE?

1. A_A_ BERRY
2. _L__KBERRY
3. BL__BERRY
4. G_J_ BERRY
5. N__I BERRY
6. R_S_BERRY
7. S_RA_BERRY

# FIND THE SUPERFOODS

```
C M R K B F A S L H H O P O H
O U O V D A J B R E E H I R I
C D U R E U X C T X Y E S T Q
O J T G I O D Y L T W Q N N U
N U K V O N D F O D A V Q A P
U R Z I G L G P O X X T W L Y
T V E P U O L A T N A C P I T
L N P J H A E E I H S A M C E
O R I D N P L U B H V V E K S
G W I K K S E A M O S S H D O
M C T C I P P F C Y T I K T J
U O I C A R R A H G A R E A M
N H J R Z X D J G X M Y O R U
C S D Y A O N I U Q C X G P S
P M O T Y L Z T I F A U X O G
```

## LOOK FOR THESE HEALTHY FOODS IN THE WORD SEARCH!

| QUINOA | PHYTOPLANKTON | MORINGA | CANTALOUPE |
|---|---|---|---|
| CILANTRO | SEAMOSS | COCONUT | CHICKPEA |
| REISHI | HEMP | AVOCADO | PORTOBELLO |